_ne_

a Book?

VIRGINIA WOOLF

WORLD BOOK DAY
SPECIAL 2021

RENARD PRESS

RENARD PRESS LTD

Kemp House
152–160 City Road
London EC1V 2NX
United Kingdom
info@renardpress.com
020 8050 2928

www.renardpress.com

How Should One Read a Book? first published in 1925
This edition first published by Renard Press Ltd in 2021

Edited text © Renard Press Ltd, 2021
Extra Material © Renard Press Ltd, 2021

Cover design by Will Dady
Biographical Note edited by Tom Conaghan

Printed and hand-bound in the United Kingdom on Olin
Smooth (FSC certified) archival grade paper

ISBN: 978-1-913724-47-4

9 8 7 6 5 4 3 2 1

HOW SHOULD ONE

READ A BOOK?[1]

---

1 This essay is based on a paper read at a school.

IN THE FIRST PLACE, I want to emphasise the note of interrogation at the end of my title. Even if I could answer the question for myself, the answer would apply only to me, and not to you. The only advice, indeed, that one person can give another about reading is to take no advice, to follow your own instincts, to use your own reason, to come to your own conclusions. If this is agreed between us, then I feel at liberty to put forward a few ideas and suggestions, because you will not allow them to fetter that independence which is the most important quality that a reader can possess. After all, what laws can be laid down about books? The Battle of Waterloo was certainly fought on a certain day; but is *Hamlet* a better play than *Lear?* Nobody can say. Each must decide that question for himself. To admit authorities, however heavily furred and gowned, into our libraries and let them tell us how to read, what to read, what value to place upon what we read, is to destroy the spirit of freedom which is the breath of those sanctuaries. Everywhere else we may be bound by laws and conventions – there we have none.

But to enjoy freedom, if the platitude is pardonable, we have, of course, to control ourselves. We must not squander our powers, helplessly and ignorantly, squirting half the house in order to water a single rose bush; we must train them, exactly and powerfully, here on the very spot. This, it may be, is one of the first difficulties that faces us in a library. What is 'the very spot'? There may well seem to be nothing but a conglomeration and huddle of confusion. Poems and novels, histories and memoirs, dictionaries and blue books;* books written in all languages by men and women of all tempers, races and ages jostle each other on the shelf. And outside the donkey brays, the women gossip at the pump, the colts gallop across the fields. Where are we to begin? How are we to bring order into this multitudinous chaos and so get the deepest and widest pleasure from what we read?

It is simple enough to say that since books have classes – fiction, biography, poetry – we should separate them and take from each what it is right that each should give us. Yet few people ask from books what books can give us. Most commonly we come to books with blurred and divided minds, asking of fiction that it shall be true, of poetry that it shall be false, of biography that it shall be flattering, of history that it shall enforce our own prejudices. If we could banish all such preconceptions when we read, that would be an admirable beginning. Do not dictate to your author; try to become him. Be his fellow worker and accomplice. If you hang back, and reserve and criticise at first, you are preventing yourself from getting the fullest possible value from what you read. But if you open your mind as widely as possible, then signs and hints of almost imperceptible fineness, from the twist and turn of the first sentences, will bring you into the presence of a human being unlike any other. Steep yourself in this, acquaint yourself with this, and soon you will find that your author is giving you, or attempting to give you, something far more definite. The thirty-two chapters of a novel – if we consider how to read a novel first – are an attempt to make something as formed and controlled as a building: but words are more impalpable than bricks; reading is a longer and more complicated process than seeing. Perhaps the quickest way to understand the elements of what a novelist is doing is not to read, but to write – to make your own experiment with the dangers and difficulties of words. Recall, then, some event that has left a distinct impression on you – how at the corner of the street, perhaps, you passed two people talking. A tree shook; an electric light danced; the tone of the talk was comic, but also tragic; a whole vision, an entire conception, seemed contained in that moment.

But when you attempt to reconstruct it in words, you will find that it breaks into a thousand conflicting impressions. Some must be subdued; others emphasised; in the process you will lose, probably, all grasp upon the emotion itself. Then turn from your blurred and littered pages to the opening pages of some great novelist – Defoe, Jane Austen, Hardy. Now you will be better able to appreciate their mastery. It is not merely that we are in the presence of a different person – Defoe, Jane Austen, or Thomas Hardy – but that we are living in a different world. Here, in *Robinson Crusoe*, we are trudging a plain high road; one thing happens after another; the fact and the order of the fact is enough. But if the open air and adventure mean everything to Defoe, they mean nothing to Jane Austen. Hers is the drawing room, and people talking, and by the many mirrors of their talk revealing their characters. And if, when we have accustomed ourselves to the drawing room and its reflections, we turn to Hardy, we are once more spun round. The moors are round us and the stars are above our heads. The other side of the mind is now exposed – the dark side that comes uppermost in solitude, not the light side that shows in company. Our relations are not towards people, but towards nature and destiny. Yet different as these worlds are, each is consistent with itself. The maker of each is careful to observe the laws of his own perspective, and however great a strain they may put upon us they will never confuse us, as lesser writers so frequently do, by introducing two different kinds of reality into the same book. Thus to go from one great novelist to another – from Jane Austen to Hardy, from Peacock to Trollope, from Scott to Meredith – is to be wrenched and uprooted; to be thrown this way and then that. To read a novel is a difficult and complex art. You must be capable not only of great fineness of perception, but of great boldness of imagination if you are going to make use of all that the novelist – the great artist – gives you.

But a glance at the heterogeneous company on the shelf will show you that writers are very seldom 'great artists'; far more often a book makes no claim to be a work of art at all. These biographies and autobiographies, for example, lives of great men, of men long dead and forgotten, that stand cheek by jowl with the novels and poems: are we to refuse to read them because they are not 'art'? Or shall we read them, but read them in a different way, with a different aim? Shall we read them in the first place to satisfy that curiosity which possesses us sometimes when in the evening we linger in front of a house where the lights are lit and the blinds not yet drawn, and each floor of the house shows us a different section of human life in being? Then we are consumed with curiosity about the lives of these people – the servants gossiping, the gentlemen dining, the girl dressing for a party, the old woman at the window with her knitting. Who are they? What are they? What are their names, their occupations, their thoughts and adventures?

Biographies and memoirs answer such questions, light up innumerable such houses; they show us people going about their daily affairs, toiling, failing, succeeding, eating, hating, loving, until they die. And sometimes, as we watch, the house fades and the iron railings vanish and we are out at sea; we are hunting, sailing, fighting; we are among savages and soldiers; we are taking part in great campaigns. Or if we like to stay here in England, in London, still the scene changes; the street narrows; the house becomes small, cramped, diamond-paned and malodorous. We see a poet, Donne, driven from such a house because the walls were so thin that when the children cried their voices cut through them. We can follow him, through the paths that lie in the pages of books, to Twickenham; to Lady Bedford's Park, a famous meeting ground for nobles and poets;* and then turn

11

our steps to Wilton, the great house under the downs, and hear Sidney read the *Arcadia* to his sister;* and ramble among the very marshes and see the very herons that figure in that famous romance; and then again travel north with that other Lady Pembroke, Anne Clifford, to her wild moors, or plunge into the city and control our merriment at the sight of Gabriel Harvey* in his black velvet suit arguing about poetry with Spenser. Nothing is more fascinating than to grope and stumble in the alternate darkness and splendour of Elizabethan London. But there is no staying there. The Temples and the Swifts, the Harleys and the St Johns beckon us on; hour upon hour can be spent disentangling their quarrels and deciphering their characters; and when we tire of them we can stroll on, past a lady in black wearing diamonds, to Samuel Johnson and Goldsmith and Garrick; or cross the channel, if we like, and meet Voltaire and Diderot, Madame du Deffand;* and so back to England and Twickenham – how certain places repeat themselves, and certain names – where Lady Bedford had her park once and Pope lived later, to Walpole's home at Strawberry Hill. But Walpole introduces us to such a swarm of new acquaintances, there are so many houses to visit and bells to ring that we may well hesitate for a moment, on the Miss Berrys' doorstep, for example, when behold, up comes Thackeray;* he is the friend of the woman whom Walpole loved; so that merely by going from friend to friend, from garden to garden, from house to house, we have passed from one end of English literature to another and wake to find ourselves here again in the present, if we can so differentiate this moment from all that have gone before. This, then, is one of the ways in which we can read these lives and letters; we can make them light up the many windows of the past; we can watch the famous dead in their familiar habits and fancy sometimes that we are very close and can surprise their secrets, and sometimes we may pull out a play or a poem that they have written and see whether it reads differently in the presence of the author. But this again rouses other questions. How far, we must ask ourselves, is a book influenced by its writer's life – how far is it safe to let the man interpret the writer? How far shall we resist or give way to the sympathies and antipathies that the man himself rouses in us – so sensitive are words, so receptive of the character of the author? These are questions that press upon us when we read lives and letters, and we must answer them for ourselves, for nothing can be more fatal than to be guided by the preferences of others in a matter so personal.

But also we can read such books with another aim, not to throw light on literature, not to become familiar with famous people, but to refresh and exercise our own creative powers. Is there not an open window on the right hand of the bookcase? How delightful to stop reading and look out! How stimulating the scene is, in its unconsciousness, its irrelevance, its perpetual movement – the colts galloping round the field, the woman filling her pail at the well, the donkey throwing back his head and emitting his long, acrid moan. The greater part of any library is nothing but the record of such fleeting moments in the lives of men, women and donkeys. Every literature, as it grows old, has its rubbish heap, its record of vanished moments and forgotten lives told in faltering and feeble accents that have perished. But if you give yourself up to the delight of rubbish-reading you will be surprised – indeed you will be overcome – by the relics of human life that have been cast out to moulder. It may be one letter – but what a vision it gives! It may be a few sentences – but what vistas they suggest! Sometimes a whole story will come together with such beautiful humour and pathos and completeness that it seems as if a great novelist had been at work, yet it is only an old actor, Tate Wilkinson, remembering the strange story of Captain Jones; it is only a young subaltern serving under Arthur Wellesley and falling in love with a pretty girl at Lisbon; it is only Maria Allen letting fall her sewing in the empty drawing-room and sighing how she wishes she had taken Dr Burney's good advice and had never eloped with her Rishy.* None of this has any value; it is negligible in the extreme; yet how absorbing it is now and again to go through the rubbish heaps and find rings and scissors and broken noses buried in the huge past and try to piece them together while the colt gallops round the field, the woman fills her pail at the well and the donkey brays.

But we tire of rubbish-reading in the long run. We tire of searching for what is needed to complete the half-truth which is all that the Wilkinsons, the Bunburys* and the Maria Allens are able to offer us. They had not the artist's power of mastering and eliminating; they could not tell the whole truth even about their own lives; they have disfigured the story that might have been so shapely. Facts are all that they can offer us, and facts are a very inferior form of fiction. Thus the desire grows upon us to have done with half-statements and approximations; to cease from searching out the minute shades of human character, to enjoy the greater abstractness, the purer truth of fiction. Thus we create the mood, intense and generalised, unaware of detail, but stressed by some regular, recurrent beat, whose natural expression is poetry; and that is the time to read poetry... when we are almost able to write it.

Western wind, when wilt thou blow?
The small rain down can rain.
Christ, if my love were in my arms,
And I in my bed again!*

The impact of poetry is so hard and direct that for the moment there is no other sensation except that of the poem itself. What profound depths we visit then – how sudden and complete is our immersion! There is nothing here to catch hold of; nothing to stay us in our flight. The illusion of fiction is gradual; its effects are prepared; but who when they read these four lines stops to ask who wrote them, or conjures up the thought of Donne's house or Sidney's secretary; or enmeshes them in the intricacy of the past and the succession of generations? The poet is always our contemporary. Our being for the moment is centred and constricted, as in any violent shock of personal emotion. Afterwards, it is true, the sensation begins to spread in wider rings through our minds; remoter senses are reached; these begin to sound and to comment and we are aware of echoes and reflections. The intensity of poetry covers an immense range of emotion. We have only to compare the force and directness of

I shall fall like a tree, and find my grave,
Only remembering that I grieve*

17

with the wavering modulation of

Minutes are numbered by the fall of sands,
As by an hour glass; the span of time
Doth waste us to our graves, and we look on it;
An age of pleasure, revelled out, comes home
At last, and ends in sorrow; but the life,
Weary of riot, numbers every sand,
Wailing in sighs, until the last drop down,
So to conclude calamity in rest,*

or place the meditative calm of

        whether we be young or old,
  Our destiny, our being's heart and home,
  Is with infinitude, and only there;
  With hope it is, hope that can never die,
  Effort, and expectation, and desire,
  And something evermore about to be*

beside the complete and inexhaustible love-
liness of

  The moving moon went up the sky,
  And nowhere did abide:
  Softly she was going up,
  And a star or two beside*

= or the splendid fantasy of

> And the woodland haunter
> Shall not cease to saunter
>   When, far down some glade,
> Of the great world's burning,
> One soft flame upturning
> Seems, to his discerning,
>   Crocus in the shade,*

to bethink us of the varied art of the poet; his power to make us at once actors and spectators; his power to run his hand into character as if it were a glove, and be Falstaff or Lear; his power to condense, to widen, to state, once and for ever.

'We have only to compare' – with those words the cat is out of the bag, and the true complexity of reading is admitted. The first process, to receive impressions with the utmost understanding, is only half the process of reading; it must be completed, if we are to get the whole pleasure from a book, by another. We must pass judgement upon these multitudinous impressions; we must make of these fleeting shapes one that is hard and lasting. But not directly. Wait for the dust of reading to settle; for the conflict and the questioning to die down; walk, talk, pull the dead petals from a rose, or fall asleep. Then, suddenly, without our willing it, for it is thus that nature undertakes these transitions, the book will return, but differently. It will float to the top of the mind as a whole. And the book as a whole is different from the book received currently in separate phrases. Details now fit themselves into their places. We see the shape from start to finish; it is a barn, a pigsty or a cathedral. Now, then, we can compare book with book as we compare building with building. But this act of comparison means that our attitude has changed; we are no longer the friends of the writer, but his judges; and just as we cannot be too sympathetic as friends, so as judges we cannot be too severe. Are they not criminals, books that have wasted our time and sympathy? Are they not the most insidious enemies of society, corrupters, defilers, the writers of false books, faked books, books that fill the air with decay and disease? Let us, then, be severe in our judgements; let us compare each book with the greatest of its kind. There they hang in the mind the shapes of the books we have read solidified by the judgements we have passed on them – *Robinson Crusoe, Emma, The Return of the Native.** Compare the novels with these – even the latest and least of novels has a right to be judged with the best. And so with poetry – when the intoxication of rhythm has died down and the splendour of words has faded, a visionary shape will return to us and this must be compared with *Lear,* with *Phèdre,** with *The Prelude;* or, if not with these, with whatever is the best or seems to us to be the best in its own kind. And we may be sure that the newness of new poetry and fiction is its most superficial quality and that we have only to alter slightly, not to recast, the standards by which we have judged the old.

It would be foolish, then, to pretend that the second part of reading, to judge, to compare, is as simple as the first – to open the mind wide to the fast flocking of innumerable impressions. To continue reading without the book before you, to hold one shadow-shape against another, to have read widely enough and with enough understanding to make such comparisons alive and illuminating – that is difficult; it is still more difficult to press further and to say, 'Not only is the book of this sort, but it is of this value; here it fails; here it succeeds; this is bad; that is good'. To carry out this part of a reader's duty needs such imagination, insight and learning that it is hard to conceive any one mind sufficiently endowed; impossible for the most self-confident to find more than the seeds of such powers in himself. Would it not be wiser, then, to remit this part of reading and to allow the critics, the gowned and furred authorities of the library, to decide the question of the book's absolute value for us? Yet how impossible! We may stress the value of sympathy; we may try to sink our identity as we read. But we know that we cannot sympathise wholly or immerse ourselves wholly; there is always a demon in us who whispers, 'I hate, I love', and we cannot silence him. Indeed, it is precisely because we hate and we love that our relation with the poets and novelists is so intimate that we find the presence of another person intolerable. And even if the results are abhorrent and our judgements are wrong, still our taste, the nerve of sensation that sends shocks through us, is our chief illuminant; we learn through feeling; we cannot suppress our own idiosyncrasy without impoverishing it. But as time goes on perhaps we can train our taste; perhaps we can make it submit to some control. When it has fed greedily and lavishly upon books of all sorts — poetry, fiction, history, biography — and has stopped reading and looked for long spaces upon the variety, the incongruity of the living world, we shall find that it is changing a little; it is not so greedy, it is more reflective. It will begin to bring us not merely judgements on particular books, but it will tell us that there is a quality common to certain books. Listen, it will say, what shall we call *this*? And it will read us perhaps *Lear* and then perhaps the *Agamemnon** in order to bring out that common quality. Thus, with our taste to guide us, we shall venture beyond the particular book in search of qualities that group books together; we shall give them names, and thus frame a rule that brings order into our perceptions. We shall gain a further and a rarer pleasure from that discrimination. But as a rule only lives when it is perpetually broken by contact with the books themselves – nothing is easier and more stultifying than to make rules which exist out of touch with facts, in a vacuum – now at last, in order to steady ourselves in this difficult attempt, it may be well to turn to the very rare writers who are able to enlighten us upon literature as an art. Coleridge and Dryden and Johnson, in their considered criticism, the poets and novelists themselves in their considered sayings, are often surprisingly relevant; they light up and solidify the vague ideas that have been tumbling in the misty depths of our minds. But they are only able to help us if we come to them laden with questions and suggestions won honestly in the course of our own reading. They can do nothing for us if we herd ourselves under their authority and lie down like sheep in the shade of a hedge. We can only understand their ruling when it comes in conflict with our own and vanquishes it.

If this is so, if to read a book as it should be read calls for the rarest qualities of imagination, insight and judgement, you may perhaps conclude that literature is a very complex art and that it is unlikely that we shall be able, even after a lifetime of reading, to make any valuable contribution to its criticism. We must remain readers; we shall not put on the further glory that belongs to those rare beings who are also critics. But still we have our responsibilities as readers and even our importance. The standards we raise and the judgements we pass steal into the air and become part of the atmosphere which writers breathe as they work. An influence is created which tells upon them even if it never finds its way into print. And that influence, if it were well instructed, vigorous and individual and sincere, might be of great value now, when criticism is necessarily in abeyance; when books pass in review like the procession of animals in a shooting gallery, and the critic has only one second in which to load and aim and shoot and may well be pardoned if he mistakes rabbits for tigers, eagles for barn-door fowls, or misses altogether and wastes his shot upon some peaceful cow grazing in a further field. If behind the erratic gunfire of the press the author felt that there was another kind of criticism, the opinion of people reading for the love of reading, slowly and unprofessionally, and judging with great sympathy and yet with great severity, might this not improve the quality of his work? And if by our means books were to become stronger, richer and more varied, that would be an end worth reaching.

Yet who reads to bring about an end, however desirable? Are there not some pursuits that we practise because they are good in themselves, and some pleasures that are final? And is not this among them? I have sometimes dreamt, at least, that when the Day of Judgement dawns and the great conquerors and lawyers and statesmen come to receive their rewards – their crowns, their laurels, their names carved indelibly upon imperishable marble – the Almighty will turn to Peter and will say, not without a certain envy when he sees us coming with our books under our arms, 'Look, these need no reward. We have nothing to give them here. They have loved reading.'

NOTE ON THE TEXT

The text of this edition is based on that published in *The Second Common Reader* (1932), which is widely considered to be the authoritative text. In some instances spelling and punctuation has been silently corrected to make the text more appealing to the modern reader.

NOTES

Please note: in an effort to keep annotations on such a short text to a minimum, some of the more obvious or well-known references have been excluded.

6 *blue books*: Handbooks or guidebooks.

11 *Lady Bedford's Park… poets*: A reference to Lucy Russell, Countess of Bedford (1580–1627), who was a patron of the arts, and whose grand Twickenham Park was, as Woolf says, a meeting place for poets and nobles alike.

12 *Wilton… his sister*: Sir Philip Sidney (1554–86) wrote *The Countess of Pembroke's Arcadia* while staying with his sister Mary, the Countess of Pembroke, at Wilton House in Wiltshire in around 1577–1580.

12 *Lady Pembroke… Spenser*: The references are to diarist and patron of literature Lady Anne Clifford, Countess of Dorset, Pembroke and Montgomery (1590–1676) and to the writer Gabriel Harvey (*c*.1552–1631).

12 *Madame du Deffand*: A reference to the French patron of the arts Marie Anne de Vichy-Chamrond (1696–1780).

13 *Miss Berrys'… Thackeray*: A reference to the writer Mary Berry (1763–1852) and her sister Agnes, who were considered very close acquaintances of the writer Horace Walpole (1717–97), eventually inheriting his literary collection.

15 *Tate Wilkinson… Rishy*: The references are to the actor Tate Wilkinson (1739–1803); captain of the 1620 voyage of the *Mayflower*, Christopher Jones (*c*.1570–1622); the 1st Duke of Wellington Arthur Wellesley (1769–1852); and to three people mentioned in the writings of Fanny Burney (1752–1840).

16 *Bunburys*: A reference to the prolific writer Selina Bunbury (1802–1882).

16 *Western wind… again*: An early 16th-century song, thought to be a fragment of medieval poetry.

17 *I shall fall like a tree... grieve*: From *The Maid's Tragedy* (1717) by Francis Beaumont (1584–1616) and John Fletcher (1579–1625).

18 *Minutes are numbered... rest*: From *The Lover's Melancholy* (1629) by John Ford (1586–*c*.1639).

18 *whether we be young or old... to be*: From *The Prelude* (Book VI) by William Wordsworth (1770–1850).

18 *The moving moon... beside*: From *The Rime of the Ancient Mariner* (Part IV) by Samuel Taylor Coleridge (1772–1834).

19 *And the woodland... shade*: From 'When the World Is Burning' by Ebenezer Jones (1820–60).

21 *The Return of the Native*: The 1878 novel by Thomas Hardy (1840–1928).

21 *Phèdre*: The 1677 play by Jean Racine (1639–99).

23 *Agamemnon*: The first of the *Oresteia* trilogy, written by Aeschylus (*c*.525–*c*.456 BC).

A Biographical Note on

Virginia Woolf

Born Adeline Virginia Stephen on the 25th
of January 1882, Woolf was a Modernist
author, poet and literary critic. She is considered one of the most important writers of
the twentieth century and a pioneer in the use
of 'stream of consciousness' as a narrative
form. In 1917, she and her husband Leonard
bought a hand-printing press and set up the
Hogarth Press in their house in Richmond,
which published much of Virginia's work, as
well as those of friends and fellow luminar-
ies. She was a member of the Bloomsbury Set
– an artistic, philosophic and literary group
which included John Maynard Keynes, Roger
Fry and Lytton Strachey.

Woolf struggled with mental illness for
much of her life, and there were periods

where she was not able to write at all, and it eventually led to her tragic death.

Her legacy is vast – she left nine novels, just shy of fifty short stories, a biography, three book-length essays and countless other shorter papers, letters and journals. Today she is best remembered for her novels – in particular *To the Lighthouse* and *Mrs Dalloway* – as well as her essay *A Room of One's Own*.